BROADWAY SONGS
with a Classical Flair

15 SELECTIONS ARRANGED BY PHILLIP KEVEREN

— PIANO LEVEL —
INTERMEDIATE

ISBN 978-1-5400-3666-7

Visit Hal Leonard Online at
www.halleonard.com

Visit Phillip at
www.phillipkeveren.com

Contact us:
Hal Leonard
7777 West Bluemound Road
Milwaukee, WI 53213
Email: info@halleonard.com

In Europe, contact:
Hal Leonard Europe Limited
42 Wigmore Street
Marylebone, London, W1U 2RN
Email: info@halleonardeurope.com

In Australia, contact:
Hal Leonard Australia Pty. Ltd.
4 Lentara Court
Cheltenham, Victoria, 3192 Australia
Email: info@halleonard.com.au

PREFACE

Using classical compositional devices, these great songs from Broadway have been developed into character pieces for piano solo. The term "classical" gets tossed about widely in the world of music. In this application, my guiding goal is to fashion an arrangement that feels more like a composition created expressly for the piano.

I hope these settings will enrich your enjoyment of music in general, and the pleasure of pursuing keyboard artistry in particular.

Sincerely,

BIOGRAPHY

Phillip Keveren, a multi-talented keyboard artist and composer, has composed original works in a variety of genres from piano solo to symphonic orchestra. He gives frequent concerts and workshops for teachers and their students in the United States, Canada, Europe, Australia, and Asia. Mr. Keveren holds a B.M. in composition from California State University Northridge and a M.M. in composition from the University of Southern California.

CONTENTS

THE BELLS OF NOTRE DAME
from THE HUNCHBACK OF NOTRE DAME

Music by ALAN MENKEN
Lyrics by STEPHEN SCHWARTZ
Arranged by Phillip Keveren

DEFYING GRAVITY
from the Broadway Musical WICKED

Music and Lyrics by
STEPHEN SCHWARTZ
Arranged by Phillip Keveren

FALLING SLOWLY
from the Broadway Musical ONCE

Words and Music by GLEN HANSARD
and MARKETA IRGLOVA
Arranged by Phillip Keveren

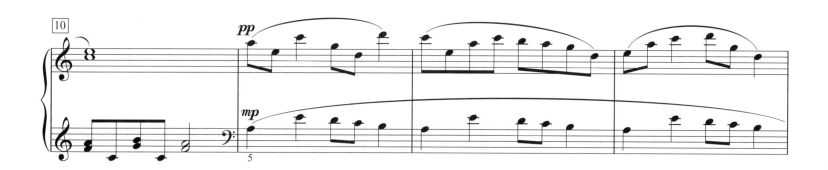

FOOLISH TO THINK
from A GENTLEMAN'S GUIDE TO LOVE & MURDER

Music by STEVEN LUTVAK
Lyrics by ROBERT L. FREEDMAN
and STEVEN LUTVAK
Arranged by Phillip Keveren

FOR FOREVER

from DEAR EVAN HANSEN

Music and Lyrics by BENJ PASEK
and JUSTIN PAUL
Arranged by Phillip Keveren

HOME
from the Broadway Musical WONDERLAND

Music by FRANK WILDHORN
Lyrics by JACK MURPHY
Arranged by Phillip Keveren

Tenderly ♩ = c. 100

With pedal

I DREAMED A DREAM

from LES MISÉRABLES

Music by CLAUDE-MICHEL SCHÖNBERG
Lyrics by ALAIN BOUBLIL, JEAN-MARC NATEL
and HERBERT KRETZMER
Arranged by Phillip Keveren

Andante, in a stately Baroque fashion ♩ = 76

Music and French Lyrics Copyright © 1980 by Editions Musicales Alain Boublil
English Lyrics Copyright © 1986 by Alain Boublil Music Ltd. (ASCAP)
This edition Copyright © 2000 by Alain Boublil Music Ltd. (ASCAP)
Mechanical and Publication Rights for the U.S.A. Administered by Alain Boublil Music Ltd. (ASCAP) c/o Spielman Koenigsberg & Parker, LLP, Richard Koenigsberg,
1675 Broadway, 20th Floor, New York, NY 10019, Tel 212-453-2500, Fax 212-453-2550, ABML@skpny.com

ME AND THE SKY
from COME FROM AWAY

Music and Lyrics by IRENE SANKOFF
and DAVID HEIN
Arranged by Phillip Keveren

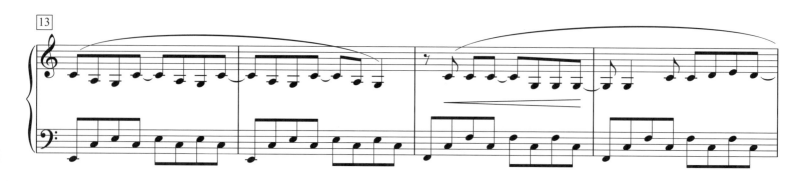

OMAR SHARIF
from THE BAND'S VISIT

Words and Music by DAVID YAZBEK
Arranged by Phillip Keveren

ONCE UPON A DECEMBER
from the Broadway Musical ANASTASIA

Words and Music by LYNN AHRENS
and STEPHEN FLAHERTY
Arranged by Phillip Keveren

SEIZE THE DAY
from NEWSIES THE MUSICAL

Music by ALAN MENKEN
Lyrics by JACK FELDMAN
Arranged by Phillip Keveren

Deeply expressive ♩ = c. 80–84

With pedal

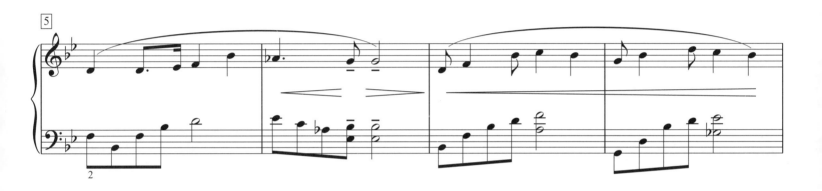

SHE USED TO BE MINE
from WAITRESS THE MUSICAL

Words and Music by SARA BAREILLES
Arranged by Phillip Keveren

SO FAR AWAY

featured in BEAUTIFUL: THE CAROLE KING MUSICAL

Words and Music by CAROLE KING
Arranged by Phillip Keveren

Poignantly, with rubato ♩ = c. 60

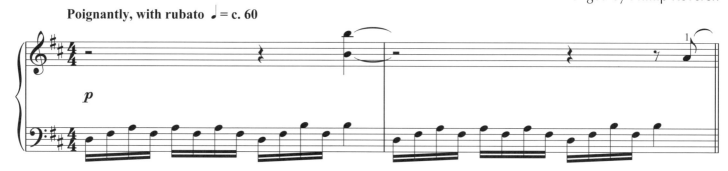

WAVING THROUGH A WINDOW

from DEAR EVAN HANSEN

Music and Lyrics by BENJ PASEK
and JUSTIN PAUL
Arranged by Phillip Keveren

YOU'LL BE BACK
from HAMILTON

Words and Music by
LIN-MANUEL MIRANDA
Arranged by Phillip Keveren

THE PHILLIP KEVEREN SERIES

PIANO SOLO

ABBA FOR CLASSICAL PIANO
00156644...$14.99
ABOVE ALL
00311024...$12.99
BACH MEETS JAZZ
00198473...$14.99
THE BEATLES
00306412...$16.99
THE BEATLES FOR CLASSICAL PIANO
00312189...$14.99
THE BEATLES – RECITAL SUITES
00275876...$19.99
BEST PIANO SOLOS
00312546...$14.99
BLESSINGS
00156601...$12.99
BLUES CLASSICS
00198656...$12.99
BROADWAY'S BEST
00310669...$14.99
A CELTIC CHRISTMAS
00310629...$12.99
THE CELTIC COLLECTION
00310549...$12.95
CELTIC SONGS WITH A CLASSICAL FLAIR
00280571...$12.99
CHRISTMAS MEDLEYS
00311414...$12.99
CHRISTMAS AT THE MOVIES
00312190...$14.99
CHRISTMAS SONGS FOR CLASSICAL PIANO
00233788...$12.99
CINEMA CLASSICS
00310607...$14.99
CLASSICAL JAZZ
00311083...$12.95
COLDPLAY FOR CLASSICAL PIANO
00137779...$15.99
DISNEY RECITAL SUITES
00249097...$16.99
DISNEY SONGS FOR CLASSICAL PIANO
00311754...$16.99
DISNEY SONGS FOR RAGTIME PIANO
00241379...$16.99
THE FILM SCORE COLLECTION
00311811...$14.99
FOLKSONGS WITH A CLASSICAL FLAIR
00269408...$12.99
GOLDEN SCORES
00233789...$14.99
GOSPEL GREATS
00144351...$12.99
GREAT STANDARDS
00311157...$12.95
THE HYMN COLLECTION
00311071...$12.99
HYMN MEDLEYS
00311349...$12.99
HYMNS IN A CELTIC STYLE
00280705...$12.99
HYMNS WITH A CLASSICAL FLAIR
00269407...$12.99
HYMNS WITH A TOUCH OF JAZZ
00311249...$12.99
JINGLE JAZZ
00310762...$14.99
BILLY JOEL FOR CLASSICAL PIANO
00175310...$15.99
ELTON JOHN FOR CLASSICAL PIANO
00126449...$15.99
LET FREEDOM RING!
00310839...$12.99

ANDREW LLOYD WEBBER
00313227...$15.99
MANCINI MAGIC
00313523...$14.99
MORE DISNEY SONGS FOR CLASSICAL PIANO
00312113...$15.99
MOTOWN HITS
00311295...$12.95
PIAZZOLLA TANGOS
00306870...$15.99
QUEEN FOR CLASSICAL PIANO
00156645...$15.99
RICHARD RODGERS CLASSICS
00310755...$15.99
SHOUT TO THE LORD!
00310699...$14.99
SONGS FROM CHILDHOOD FOR EASY CLASSICAL PIANO
00233688...$12.99
THE SOUND OF MUSIC
00119403...$14.99
SYMPHONIC HYMNS FOR PIANO
00224738...$14.99
TIN PAN ALLEY
00279673...$12.99
TREASURED HYMNS FOR CLASSICAL PIANO
00312112...$14.99
THE TWELVE KEYS OF CHRISTMAS
00144926...$12.99
YULETIDE JAZZ
00311911...$17.99

EASY PIANO

AFRICAN-AMERICAN SPIRITUALS
00310610...$10.99
CATCHY SONGS FOR PIANO
00218387...$12.99
CELTIC DREAMS
00310973...$10.95
CHRISTMAS CAROLS FOR EASY CLASSICAL PIANO
00233686...$12.99
CHRISTMAS POPS
00311126...$14.99
CLASSIC POP/ROCK HITS
00311548...$12.95
A CLASSICAL CHRISTMAS
00310769...$10.95
CLASSICAL MOVIE THEMES
00310975...$12.99
CONTEMPORARY WORSHIP FAVORITES
00311805...$14.99
DISNEY SONGS FOR EASY CLASSICAL PIANO
00144352...$12.99
EARLY ROCK 'N' ROLL
00311093...$12.99
GEORGE GERSHWIN CLASSICS
00110374...$12.99
GOSPEL TREASURES
00310805...$12.99
THE VINCE GUARALDI COLLECTION
00306821...$16.99
HYMNS FOR EASY CLASSICAL PIANO
00160294...$12.99
IMMORTAL HYMNS
00310798...$12.99
JAZZ STANDARDS
00311294...$12.99
LOVE SONGS
00310744...$12.99
THE MOST BEAUTIFUL SONGS FOR EASY CLASSICAL PIANO
00233740...$12.99
POP STANDARDS FOR EASY CLASSICAL PIANO
00233739...$12.99

RAGTIME CLASSICS
00311293...$10.95
SONGS FROM CHILDHOOD FOR EASY CLASSICAL PIANO
00233688...$12.99
SONGS OF INSPIRATION
00103258...$12.99
TIMELESS PRAISE
00310712...$12.95
10,000 REASONS
00126450...$14.99
TV THEMES
00311086...$12.99
21 GREAT CLASSICS
00310717...$12.99
WEEKLY WORSHIP
00145342...$16.99

BIG-NOTE PIANO

CHILDREN'S FAVORITE MOVIE SONGS
00310838...$12.99
CHRISTMAS MUSIC
00311247...$10.95
CLASSICAL FAVORITES
00277368...$12.99
CONTEMPORARY HITS
00310907...$12.99
DISNEY FAVORITES
00277370...$14.99
JOY TO THE WORLD
00310888...$10.95
THE NUTCRACKER
00310908...$10.99
STAR WARS
00277371...$16.99

BEGINNING PIANO SOLOS

AWESOME GOD
00311202...$12.99
CHRISTIAN CHILDREN'S FAVORITES
00310837...$12.99
CHRISTMAS FAVORITES
00311246...$10.95
CHRISTMAS TIME IS HERE
00311334...$12.99
CHRISTMAS TRADITIONS
00311117...$10.99
EASY HYMNS
00311250...$12.99
EVERLASTING GOD
00102710...$10.99
JAZZY TUNES
00311403...$10.95

PIANO DUET

CLASSICAL THEME DUETS
00311350...$10.99
HYMN DUETS
00311544...$12.99
PRAISE & WORSHIP DUETS
00311203...$12.99
STAR WARS
00119405...$14.99
WORSHIP SONGS FOR TWO
00253545...$12.99

Visit **www.halleonard.com**
for a complete series listing.

Prices, contents, and availability subject to change without notice.

PIANO DUETS
IN THE PHILLIP KEVEREN SERIES

1 PIANO, 4 HANDS

THE CHRISTMAS VARIATIONS

Eight classic carol settings expertly arranged for piano duet by Phillip Keveren. Includes: Angels We Have Heard on High • Ding Dong! Merrily on High! • God Rest Ye Merry, Gentlemen • I Saw Three Ships • Joy to the World • Lo, How a Rose E'er Blooming • Still, Still, Still • We Wish You a Merry Christmas.
00126452 Piano Duet............$12.99

PRAISE & WORSHIP DUETS

Eight worshipful duets by Phillip Keveren: As the Deer • Awesome God • Give Thanks • Great Is the Lord • Lord, I Lift Your Name on High • Shout to the Lord • There Is a Redeemer • We Fall Down.
00311203 Piano Duet............$12.99

CLASSICAL THEME DUETS

Eight beloved masterworks masterfully arranged as early intermediate duets by Phillip Keveren. Includes: Bizet – Habanera • Borodin – Polovetsian Dance • Grieg – In the Hall of the Mountain King • Vivaldi – The Four Seasons ("Autumn") • and more.
00311350 Easy Piano Duets...$10.99

SACRED CHRISTMAS DUETS

Phillip Keveren has arranged eight beloved Christmas songs into duets perfect for holiday recitals or services. Includes: The First Noel • Go, Tell It on the Mountain • Hark! the Herald Angels Sing • It Came upon the Midnight Clear • O Come, All Ye Faithful • O Come, O Come, Emmanuel • O Holy Night • Silent Night.
00294755 Piano Duet............$12.99

GOSPEL DUETS

Eight inspiring hymns arranged by Phillip Keveren for one piano, four hands, including: Church in the Wildwood • His Eye Is on the Sparrow • In the Garden • Just a Closer Walk with Thee • The Old Rugged Cross • Shall We Gather at the River? • There Is Power in the Blood • When the Roll Is Called up Yonder.
00295099 Piano Duet $12.99

STAR WARS

Eight intergalactic arrangements of *Star Wars* themes for late intermediate to early advanced piano duet, including: Across the Stars • Cantina Band • Duel of the Fates • The Imperial March (Darth Vader's Theme) • Princess Leia's Theme • Star Wars (Main Theme) • The Throne Room (And End Title) • Yoda's Theme.
00119405 Piano Duet $14.99

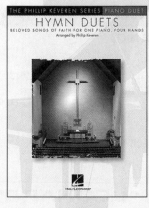

HYMN DUETS

12 beloved songs of faith: All Creatures of Our God and King • All Hail the Power of Jesus' Name • Fairest Lord Jesus • Holy, Holy, Holy • I Surrender All • Immortal, Invisible • It Is Well with My Soul • Joyful, Joyful, We Adore Thee • A Mighty Fortress Is Our God • O Sacred Head, Now Wounded • Praise to the Lord, the Almighty • Rejoice, the Lord Is King.
00311544 Piano Duet $12.99

WORSHIP SONGS FOR TWO

Eight worship favorites arranged for one piano, four hands by Phillip Keveren. Songs include: Amazing Grace (My Chains Are Gone) • Cornerstone • Forever (We Sing Hallelujah) • Great I Am • In Christ Alone • The Lion and the Lamb • Lord, I Need You • 10,000 Reasons (Bless the Lord).
00253545 Piano Duet $12.99

Prices, contents, and availability subject to change without notice.

www.halleonard.com